Jacquie Murrell

LIFE SUPPORT
REHAB

Library of Congress Cataloging-in-Publication Data
Author Jacquie Murrell
LIFE SUPPORT COMPANY
"Helping others transition from resuscitation to release in all areas of life!"

www.lifesupportmurrell.webs.com
317-886-0296
1-888-689-3066 ext 2
www.facebook.com/jacquiemurrell

Anthony KaDarrell Thigpen,
Publisher
Literacy in Motion Publications

Life Support, Rehab
Series, Part II
ISBN: 978-0-9904440-8-4
1. Christians - Religious Life/Self-Help
Printed in the United States of America

Published by
Literacy in Motion
PO BOX 7186
Chandler, AZ 85246
posttribune@hotmail.com
KaDarrell@sbcglobal.net

Jacquie Murrell

DEDICATION

To every man, woman and teenager who feels like the damages of your pain, hurt, suffering and brokenness is beyond repair; like you have every reason to give up, throw in the towel and die; know that there is nothing in this world that God cannot do. Earth has no sorrow or pain that heaven cannot feel or heal.

Live by the "I AM" factor; always knowing, trusting and believing that you are everything God says you are and called you to be. Allow your faith to cancel the synthetic fear created by the seemingly big obstacles the enemy tries to destroy you with. He will always be overpowered and conquered by an even bigger God who is the source of your every need. You must face it in order for Him to fix it. Don't ever forget there is nothing you can do that will keep Him from loving you and forgiving you. He is there to pick you up no matter how many times you fall.

To my friends; Mr. & Mrs. Woods, Mr. & Mrs. Coleman, Chandre Lee, Stacey Taylor; thank you for loving me, being there when I needed help the most, pushing me and encouraging me through every single obstacle, mistake and lesson to help me through the process of finding, healing, liking and loving me.

Life Support Rehab

TABLE OF CONTENT

Preface

DETERMINATION

But if we hope for that we see not, then do we with patience wait for it. Likewise the Spirit also helpeth our infirmities: for we know not what we should pray for as we ought: but the Spirit itself maketh intercession for us with groanings which cannot be uttered. And he that searcheth the hearts knoweth what is the mind of the Spirit, because he maketh intercession for the saints according to the will of God. And we know that all things work together for good to them that love God, to them who are the called according to his purpose **(Romans 8:25-28).**

This book is the second of a 3-part series designed to be a motivational and teaching guide. Learn how to recognize your role in your circumstances, identify the consistent habits, decisions and behaviors that are a result of your unwanted outcomes. This book will help you execute a plan to rebuild your life from the inside out.

Please bear with me as I allow transparency to enlighten, encourage and empower individuals and families. I want to help readers who are experiencing obstacles that seem too big to overcome by sharing some very intimate details of my life. I hope to share stories that most people can identify with, as well as offer some practical solutions and exercises to utilize through the *Rehab* phase of healing and rebuilding. This book covers the many relapses of my *Rehab* and tells the story about how I faced some of life's greatest struggles and made some of life's dumbest decisions, yet I pushed on relentlessly through them all. From one bad mistake and decision to another and from vicious cycle to vicious cycle, I had every reason to quit. I possessed an undying spirit. I never gave up and always knew that God had something great in store for me. I didn't care about what others thought or what they would say. The third and last book in this series will be "I'm Possible." I will give readers the finale of my *Rehab* phase depicting how I launched into everything God had waiting for me. It will also give practical tips on how to form and implement a plan to walk into your purpose experiencing liberation and prosperity. It is also a living testament of how God can take a total mess and turn it into a powerful message.

It was through hard work, determination, faith, grace, and mercy that I overcame. Now I am able to walk in victory. God can do the same thing for you. He will fulfill His promise to you and complete the work that He started in your life.

.

Chapter 1

MENTAL PREPARATION

For God hath not given us a spirit of fear; but of power, and love, and of a sound mind **(2 Timothy 1:7).**

There should come a time when you get sick and tired of being sick and tired. Don't keep doing the same things expecting different results. When you get fed up with the nonsense of life, determination overrides fear and you'll switch gears. At that point in life you'll make up in your mind that you must acquire better. Sometimes, it takes almost losing your mind to realize your decisions have caused you to willingly participate in a vicious cycle that is destroying your ability to see, hear and think clearly. When you cannot see yourself, hear God and think, in order to follow instructions, you keep yourself bound and limited to what you can do and where you can go. It is imperative that you relinquish control and allow God to take the wheel. So many of us are telling God we want Him to be our co-pilot, instead of just being content as a passenger. Living life with this mindset will cause you to experience "mayday after mayday." You will never be able to move to a different destination, always spiraling downward and out of control. You must first be willing to see all of you.

Now that we have taken time to look at some underlying issues that contribute to our current behaviors, we are ready to begin our journey into *Rehab*. This journey starts with our thought processes, decision-making, and other internal battles. Failed social relationships also hinder our ability to be successful in every aspect of life and society. Rehab will repair the foundation so that we can begin rebuilding our lives.

I left off in the first part of this series, Surviving Life's Worse

Challenges, telling you about how I went into the divorce process. Perhaps you remember I told you I went through a program in the church to help overcome the sexual abuse and brokenness I endured as a child? This program helped me a lot, but I still wasn't completely healed from it and the divorce is where I began my journey to hard-core relentless rehab. Now, let's go to work!

The divorce had taken a toll on me mentally, physically, emotionally and spiritually. My two children and I had moved in with my mother-in-law. I had to apply for welfare, as I was not receiving any child support. I was embarrassed and ashamed. I had to do whatever it took to make sure my children had everything they needed. It took me about a year to get on my feet, get a job, and finally move out on my own for the very first time in my life. During this time, my ex-husband and I were in constant battle with one another. The reality was I had just become a full time single mother. We argued and fought and went back and forth sexually for a long while. I began allowing my anger to get the best of me. I tried running him over with my car. Had it not been for his quick reaction, he would have been severely injured. I did not like the person I was becoming, but the pain I was feeling only added to everything that was still deeply rooted in me. I trusted him and I felt like he turned around and did to me what everyone else had done. My mind became the devil's playground so that the enemy could have his way in order to try and finish me off.

I can remember the pain I felt knowing my marriage was over and that I would be raising our children by myself. I was full of anger, sorrow and bitterness and now even more prideful as I didn't want anyone getting close to me or doing anything for me. I was so scared and fragile at that point. In my mind, it was me against the world and I chose to do it all on my own or at least try to.

I listened to the same sermon for 4 months straight every single day entitled "It's a Spiritual Battle." I was trying to keep my mind from going into a mental breakdown again causing my emotions and thoughts to get the best of me. I was determined to make it no matter what. Yes, there were days I cried all day and night. I begged God to make the pain and hurt go away. Suicide crossed my mind again, but I never let it get the best of me. I started asking myself what it was about me that he hated so much. Why would he chase me and put so much effort into making me his wife just to turn around and humiliate and mistreat me. I felt like one half of me died. It was like the pain would never end and at times it felt so unbearable. I knew that I had to do something out the box to get through this because just holding it in and sucking it up was not going to cut it this time. So, I continued listening to the sermon.

The more I listened to the sermon, the more I realized I was in a spiritual battle. I knew I had to get closer to God somehow. I realized my ex-husband had become my god in a way. This was the first thing God showed me about my own character and my role in the situation. I put God second to him and for that I repented. I wanted to experience the love I so desperately needed for so long. It seemed no mater how much I searched I could never find it. I was looking everywhere except in the right place. I was still broken from all of the pain from my childhood when I met him so I really had

This was the first thing God showed me about my own character and my role in the situation.

no business jumping into a relationship, let alone a marriage. I wasn't ready emotionally, mentally or spiritually to endure the things that sometimes occur in marriage. So, here I was broken even more. The stitches that I put in place when I began the counseling in the church were busted wide open causing more trauma.

I noticed that singing his praises took me to a place I had never gone when I was by myself. I began to sing myself into His presence and invite Him in. I wanted God to saturate my atmosphere and begin an intimate exchange of communication. I remember laying prostrate in the bathroom (my secret place) crying my eyes out about how sorry I was and how I needed Him to change me, love me, guide me, comfort me and take the pain away so that I could forgive. There were a few times I could literally feel something touch my shoulder and instantly the tears would subside and a peace would come over me. I knew then for sure that God was real. Reconnecting with the source that provides the resource was the key to beginning a long excruciating, yet possible journey of healing and deliverance.

While I experienced God's presence, I still did not understand how to tap into His spirit that lived in me. I needed to know how to stay connected to the source. It was a difficult struggle learning how to master this. This left a crack wide enough for the enemy to come in and tempt me into relapse. My weak moments, habits and hang-ups caused me to do some things, make some bad decisions and mistakes that would make each phase of rehab even more difficult.

REFLEX: An involuntary/automatic response to a stimulus.

I had run into an old friend from high school at work. Mark was his name. I began talking to this young man and we began to date. I explained that I was going through a divorce and to my surprise; he too had been recently divorced.

At this point, I am trying to stay focused on trying to get over the pain and keep my mind regulated. Meanwhile, new attention from another man and the interest from my ex-husband now have me getting ready to behave in ways I know are not right and especially for my children. I am beginning to relapse. I began to become angry all over again and started to think about how I tried my best to do the right thing. That was the thanks I got. So I decided I would get back at him, which is something that is usually out of my character. I was struggling to be rational in my thinking and to do what was right. I was having an extremely hard time getting over it, especially with all of the past hurt and abuse resurfacing. I had been so used to just holding everything in. I allowed people to walk all over me. I had done that for so long and suddenly I was fed up. I tried very hard to fight against the urge for revenge. Deep within I wanted to make him hurt just as much as I was. I loved him. Everything that was happening just felt unfair. I decided I wasn't going to church for a while and would start doing my own thing. It seemed like the people who did everything they were big and bad enough to do were living a happy life. On the other hand, I was miserable, despite how nice I tried to be. This was my first relapse during my rehab.

I had finally moved into an apartment of my own and had a vehicle. I was doing well, but I still was not comfortable or content. Two weeks after moving into my apartment I still hadn't unpacked. The apartment had a severe roach problem. I moved in with Mark until they fixed the pest problem at my apartment. Mark was sweet and very attentive, but he was talking about marriage too soon for me. I wasn't anywhere near ready to remarry that soon.

I asked my apartment manager to let me out of my lease if they weren't going to fix the problem. They said they were working on it and I continued to stay with Mark. Another couple from church kind of took me under their wing. They were an awesome example of what God can do in a marriage. We will call them Mr. and Mrs. Williams. Mrs. Williams was and still is a great woman of God. Mrs. Williams contacted me and told me that something in her spirit was telling her that something about Mark wasn't right. She instructed me not to stay there anymore.

It turned out she was right. Mark began staying out all night and was dating another woman. One day, I came home and all of my things were removed from his house. He had taken them back to my apartment. He told me that he was sorry and that he would be going away for a long time but wouldn't tell me why. I began searching and found out that he was getting ready to serve time in a federal prison. Looking back, I noticed that God stepped in once again by using Mrs. Williams who also took my children and me into her home until I got back on my feet. Once again, I was hurt

This was the second time I realized my behavior played a role in my circumstances.

on top of more hurt and I had to find a different outlet before I lost it again. Also, looking back, I noticed I had no business entertaining him. This was the second time I realized my behavior played a role in my circumstances. It was almost like my need to be wanted and loved overpowered my ability to stay focused on completing the healing process. I needed to learn how to love my own self first.

Mr. and Mrs. Williams helped me out a lot with my children and were very blunt with me. I didn't want to hear what they were saying sometimes. Although I knew what they were saying was right. They talked to both JR and I, and things cooled down for a little while and we began seeing each other again. However, I knew JR had been seeing someone else at the same time. Looking back, I still had not grasped the fact that I no longer had to allow myself to be used. I didn't know who I was, what I was, or whose I was. I settled because any attention and smooth words comforted my pain, loneliness and need to feel loved. So I would go have sex with him not realizing I was still holding on. I equated his physical desires to love.

After a while, I became numb to the disrespect that began taking place. Once again, I was humiliated with his words and actions. It was only a matter of time before I snapped back out of it and tried to get back to work. It became evident that I would not be able to start off walking during rehab, but work on my cognitive skills while crawling before walking.

CHAPTER 1 LESSON

The first thing we must realize is when starting the rehab healing process, we cannot just dive into it as if it will happen instantly. When taking the time to figure out where to start just as I did, understand that you must find a way to get back into God's presence. We must stay connected to the source that will regulate our thinking, comfort our loneliness, ease the pain and wipe away the tears. When you begin this process, understand the first thing God will show you is you. Be prepared to see your ugly truth. We must also be prepared to accept people He sends to help us along the way. He knows what you went through and endured. He understands your pain and He knows who inflicted it, but He will show you your condition, your participation in the matter and the lessons that need to be learned from it. People will usually be placed along your journey to be blunt with you concerning your actions, behaviors, etc. You will know when they are doing it out of love and it will be uncomfortable, but know they are not looking down on you or judging you. Oftentimes, they too have been where you are and are equipped with the knowledge to help you along the way. Understand there are times that you will relapse, but the key is to never give up and keep trying. Your mental or emotional state will be the hardest to overcome, as they will need ongoing therapy.

As you have read, I still had the mentality of a lost and broken individual. I still allowed myself to be used and made decisions that kept me from being able to move forward in the healing process. Due to my loneliness and need to be loved I made poor decisions. I wasn't quite grasping the fact that I was experiencing an artificial love. The emotionally high moments never really filled that void, it just pacified it for a very short period. While I had never been vengeful and was open to love others, I also realized that the blows I had sustained caused a short circuit. Pain affected my thinking and behavior, altering my perception of people. This dysfunction ultimately effected how I viewed men especially, which caused me to not love myself. If I loved myself, I would not have subjected myself to such things and behaviors. As a result of not loving self, I couldn't love anyone. I knew this could not happen without forgiveness first of myself and others. I would have to learn how to forgive over and over and over.

QUESTIONS:

1. What is being revealed to you about you and your current condition?

_____

_____

_____

_____

2. If applicable, how did you participate in the matter and what is the lesson that has been revealed to you?

_____

_____

_____

_____

ACTIVITY

Once you answer the questions above, meditate on them and see if you recognize what has been revealed to you about you. Pay attention to the timeline and only focus on what God is trying to show you, whether it be through another person talking to you, a dream, a scripture, etc.

Get a piece of paper or use a laptop and draw a timeline of your decisions and behaviors and the emotions that followed so you can see the ups and downs or digression in your behavior. Start from as far back as you would like and work your way up to the point where you are now. In order for you to see self clearly and identify the things God is showing you, complete honesty is a must. This allows you to even further be mindful of where the cracks are in your foundation. Things will begin to make sense. Your timeline can be set up as detailed as you would like or even in a different format, but you may want to add the year associated with each event or month/year just so you can actually see your progress.

As you can see in my timeline example below, I started with marriage because it was my first decision as an adult on my own after being aware of the roots of why I thought and acted the way I did as discussed in the first book. There are many more decisions I could add but this is just an example. Notice how my emotions and behaviors are still the same in both decision-making events. How long do you think I stayed this way? What will be addressed first and healed? Anger? Bitterness? Pay attention to your timeline and add as you go, even adding your good decisions to help you in your rehab and see how your behavior and emotions begin to change. I guarantee that once you understand who you are and are wrapped tightly in God's love, things like forgiveness will be like second nature and so much more gets easier when faced with events and circumstances that come to make you stronger.

JOURNAL ENTRY SAMPLE

MARRIAGE	1. DECISION- Got married and wasn't emotionally, spiritually or mentally ready 2. BEHAVIOR- Loving, kind, happy, submissive only to an extent, not very affectionate, forgiving. I became wrapped up in him, accepted continuous infidelity and verbal/emotional abuse (passive), depressed, suicidal, reckless 3. EMOTIONS- hurt, angry, bitter, resentful
DIVORCE	1. DECISION- Followed my head and not my heart and signed divorce papers 2. BEHAVIOR- vengeful, homicidal, sporadic, unreasonable, unforgiving 3. EMOTIONS- angry, hurt, bitter, resentful, unworthy, less than

Now, find out what ushers you into His presence or how you can reconnect with Him on that very intimate level. Is it praying, singing, just lying prostrate and crying out to him, having a partner pray with you, listening to a sermon or encouraging words, etc. Once you do that, take everything to Him and begin the process of learning how to release it. It may take days, weeks or months, but you must release it all. You may cry it out, pray it out, talk it out with someone or a therapist, write it out, or you may even release through exercise. No matter what you do to release it, understand that the most important thing is prayer. Talk to God daily on top of your other forms of release. It doesn't have to be an elegant and long prayer. Talk to him as if you were talking to a friend and be honest with God because He already knows anyway but He longs for that relationship with you. Let Him be who He is for you.

NOTE: Make sure your are writing in your journal or recording your thoughts. Get it out.

STUDY SCRIPTURES:

John 14: 26-27

Psalm 31:1-2

Psalm 126:5

Chapter 2

PERCEPTION

The meaning the brain attributes to sensory input.

By whom also we have access by faith into this grace wherein we stand, and rejoice in hope the glory of God. And not only so, but we glory in tribulations also; knowing that tribulation worketh patience; And patience, experience; and experience, hope; And hope maketh not ashamed; because the love of God is shed abroad in our hearts by the Holy Ghost which is given unto us **(Romans 5:2-5).**

Often times, we confuse the season of reaping with the season of tests. We tend to blame others and the enemy for everything. Indeed, the enemy does cause disaster, tries to get us to fall, and give up when our faith is tested. However, sometimes we experience great loss and suffering due to our own decisions and sowing of bad seeds. When this happens, we must reap what we have sown. The awesome thing about reaping what we sow is that even when we sow negativity, grace and mercy has the ability to protect us from reaping what we should. This is God's way of saying, "I have to put you on punishment, but I am going to give you another chance to get it right. While you are going through this season, I will still make sure you have what you need to survive." We are His children and like our own children, He loves us unconditionally.

I had begun to try to pick up the pieces and focus more on my children and myself. I was determined to conquer the depression, anger, bitterness, low self-esteem, pride and so many other elements of defeat. I thought about my children and I didn't want them thinking I was handling these difficult and heart wrenching situations badly. I began going back to church and trying to learn how to stay connected to God and not let go of His hand.

Shortly after moving in with Mr. and Mrs. Williams, I lost my job. This added to the stress, but I remained determined. I found another job, but the weekend before the Monday I was supposed to start, my car was repossessed. I couldn't afford to pay to get it back because the future job only paid minimum wage – and it was part-time. My checks were only about $120 a week after taxes. I know what you're probably thinking, "How is she going to support two children off of that?" You are right. It was very little. In addition, my monthly welfare was only $288. On the other hand, something was better than nothing. I was now in another bind on top of everything else. It seemed like there was a domino effect happening again.

I started riding the bus. I lived on the side of town where bus stops were far away from the subdivision. I had to catch 10 buses daily to get my children to daycare and go to work. I woke up every morning at 4 a.m. and was on the first bus at 5:30 a.m. and didn't get back home until 11:00 p.m. I walked over a mile every morning just to get to the bus stop. I had to catch so many buses with connecting routes. Now imagine getting two small children ready at 4 a.m., getting a double stroller, blankets, umbrella, coats, diaper bag and snacks all together every morning and walking over a mile to the 1st bus stop no matter the weather. That didn't even include the rest of the walking I had to do throughout the day.

For about the first 3 days I started to complain. Afterward, I noticed how the walk kept me fit. It was also my time of reflection. One morning on my way to the bus stop, the scripture Matthew 25:21 dropped in my spirit; *"His lord said unto him, Well done, thou good and faithful servant; thou hast been faithful over a few things, I will make thee ruler over many things: enter thou into the joy of thy lord"* (KJV). At that moment a smile came across my face and a peace came over me that cancelled out the fear, worry and stress. When the bus arrived, the bus driver, who now knew I was a regular, took my stroller like he did every morning and helped the children and myself get on the bus. I started seeing God in everything good and perfect. He didn't have to unbuckle his seatbelt and get up to help us every morning, but he did it with a smile. At the very next stop every morning, there was a man in a wheelchair with no legs that the bus driver helped onto the bus. The man greeted me with a smile and I smiled back. I had to hold back tears thinking, "Here I am broken, with two children, no car and walking to the bus stop complaining, yet this man doesn't even have legs. How dare I complain when I cannot only walk to the bus stop, but I am able to step on and off the bus?" What a blessing! I decided that I would no longer complain but choose to try and find the blessings of God even in the middle of my tests, trials and lessons. That was the day I learned how to praise Him anyhow no matter my circumstances.

Some people knew what I was going through and looked at me oddly. Some even asked me how I was able to smile even still. All I could do was tell them that the only way I knew how to stay sane amid my difficulties is to thank and praise God. I had not perfected this at all at this point, but I was trying as I began to understand that no matter what mistakes I made and no matter what I endured, I was strong enough to get through it with God. The more I looked for Him in the midst of it all, the greater my faith became. They may have been waiting on me to make the same mistakes again. I knew that no matter how many times I fell, I was going to succeed no matter how long it took. It was then that I began to form the understanding that God's opinion of me was the only opinion that really mattered.

MODERATE ASSIST: *Level of assistance with mobility is 50/50 between God's vessel and individual.*

I continued to move forward and work towards focusing on my job, caring for my children, and trying to rebuild my life. I continued catching all those buses and looking for better job opportunities on the weekends without complaining. I lost the part-time job I was working and found a better job within about a month. This worked even better for me. I ended up moving out of Mr. and Mrs. Williams' home and moved in with a girlfriend. She was also going through a divorce. We lived with her for over a month. I was able to save enough money to get an apartment and we were on our own for the very first time and I loved it. I was able to obtain daycare assistance from the state and no longer had to pay for daycare out of pocket. It was hard, but I did it. Shortly after moving, I picked up a part-time evening job as well. I worked two jobs, took care of my children, styled hair and sewed clothing as a side hustle and began thinking about going back to school. I wanted to get a cosmetology license. I already had a license in alterations and tailoring. For the first time I felt a little freedom, like I was really going to make it. After doing well and gaining my balance, I had the pastor come over and bless my apartment.

Once I got settled in, my ex-husband started popping up at my apartment again after I told him I was doing just fine without him. Sometimes we would argue about the marriage and about the different people we were entertaining. This became a frequent ritual. We just couldn't leave each other alone as hard as we tried. I guess it was the love I still had for him as everything was still kind of fresh. The visits from him started making me lose focus once again. I started falling back into the trap of the same cycle and the moment I felt let down and betrayed, I went back into my bitter and angry behavior. I took 3 steps forward and got knocked 2 steps back. This is the third time I noticed I was relapsing.

> I took 3 steps forward and got knocked 2 steps back, this is the third time I noticed I was relapsing.

The weather began to get very cold. It was now late fall, early winter of 2006-2007. I made sure I took lots of blankets with me even though I had my children bundled up in their stroller along with everything else they may have needed in their bag. It was a lot to carry on and off the bus but we made it happen every day and they were excited to ride the bus. They were too young to understand the reason we were riding the bus, but knowing they enjoyed it and thought it was fun, made me feel even better. As the weather got worse, the different bus drivers and regular riders would help the children and myself on-and-off the bus from folding and unfolding the stroller to taking the bags and blankets daily. People didn't have to be so nice but I saw it as God extending a little favor, grace, and mercy towards me. Slowly but surely, God was turning everything around for me. I wasn't perfect. I'm still not perfect. I make many mistakes, but I was trying hard to get it right.

I guess God saw me trying and loved me enough to look beyond my faults and meet more of my needs. One day JR's mother called me and asked me if I had been able to purchase a car. I told her no. She responded and said, "Well you have one now." I said, "What are you talking about?" She said, "I came home and here comes my husband pulling up in a red car. I asked him, whose car is that? He said he bought it for you and the kids because it was too cold for you to be catching the bus with then babies." I began to cry silently on the phone listening to her speak. She said he paid for it with cash in full and I just had to make arrangements with him to pay him back for it later. I was totally speechless. I just began to cry some more, thank God. She came to pick the kids and me up. They gave me the keys to my new Chrysler Concorde. Words could not express how grateful I was. I was nobody, but the ex-wife of their son

In spite of my consistent mistakes and wrong decisions, he looked beyond my faults.

and mother of their grandchildren. They were not obligated to do anything of the sort, but God saw otherwise. I definitely saw God in their kindness that day. In spite of my consistent mistakes and wrong decisions, he looked beyond my faults.

In the late winter of 2007, I was working two jobs and taking care of my children and things were looking up. I was doing pretty good mentally and trying to keep it together emotionally and attend church. My mother-in-law would call and check on me almost every other day. She insisted I spend more time with my children and quit one job, but I expressed to her that I had to do whatever it took to make sure we had what we needed. I wasn't receiving any child support from her son. Shortly after, JR and I started at it again. We were trying so hard to get along and mend the relationship at least to the point where we could be cordial for the kids. Unfortunately, we still had not arrived at that point yet. I ended up cutting all communication with him for a while. That anger and bitterness started to get a little out of control again. I was determined I would try my best to stay on track and not lose focus. He was in my head and heart though. It seemed like anything negative or hurtful coming from him would send me over the top. Whenever he was sweet, it caused me to feel like the most special person in the world. Looking back, I allowed his actions and words to control my actions, thoughts and behaviors. I was truly dependent upon him emotionally and mentally. It was a recipe for disaster. This is the 4th time I saw myself about to relapse depending upon the validation of someone else because I still could not see me for myself, but i caught it this time.

> **This is the 4th time i saw myself about to relapse depending upon the validation of someone else because I still could not see me for myself, but I caught it this time.**

CHAPTER 2 LESSON

It is so easy to complain while going through a storm because while you are in it, the way is cloudy and dark and you cannot see a way out. Know that complaining in the midst of it doesn't make it pass any faster, nor does it keep you from experiencing the difficulties storms bring. It is important to notice when you are allowing someone to take control of you other than God. Nobody should be able to speak or act and it causes you to behave in the way they require of you. I was wrapped up in a man, rather than God, so I couldn't experience peace. Every time I thought I had peace, it was replaced with chaos, worry, anger and bitterness repeatedly. I loved him more than I loved myself, but also more than I loved God, or at least looking back, it seemed that way. I struggled to let go of what I knew was not good for me. It caused me to miss out on some blessings God had for me as well as time that could have been spent rebuilding me. Trusting that God's grace is sufficient for all of our needs is the key to getting over those people. They will never be able to give you what God can. As you read in the story above, He will send you assistance as long as you are doing your part. Healing and deliverance requires participation. He will not fix what you refuse to hand over to Him and let go of. Keeping Him first is key and thanking Him in everything, not for everything, but in everything. This approach will cause Him to bless you beyond what you deserve as well. He wants to know that you still trust Him even when it was your own decisions that caused you to be in the valley in the first place.

QUESTIONS

1.   How do you know if you are in a season of reaping or a season of testing of your faith? If you don't know, do you know how to find out? (Hint: God has the answers for that; Ask. Also see "ACTIVITY").

_____

_____

_____

2.   What is the one thing or person you cannot let go of? What is the reason for your repetitive behavior?

_____

_____

_____

ACTIVITY:

Remember the timeline you created? Go back to that and look at your decisions, behavior and emotions. Do you see any repetition? Do you have any negative progression? Okay, we are going to use that as self-motivation. What circumstances are you facing right now that are not comfortable and/or are difficult but you know you must go through them in order to get what you need and where you want to go? For me, it was job searching and working while taking my babies with me walking and riding all those buses relentlessly. It was tiresome, frustrating and difficult, but I had no choice. I was determined to make it not just for myself, but for them.

Get a full body mirror or use the sheet at the end of this chapter for this activity. Stand in the mirror and look at yourself and begin to write what you see and feel when you look at yourself on it in soap or any writing utensil that can be washed off. What is the first thing that comes to your mind when you see yourself flipped inside out in the mirror or on the sheet? Do you like what you see? Identify everything you want to get rid of in you as well as everything you want to change about your circumstances and circle them. As you go through REHAB and you see your timeline behavior getting better, start erasing those things and replacing them with what you now see.

Our ultimate goal is total liberation, not coping. Find your external motivator. Identify your complaints about the situation. Now take a piece of paper and make a list of everything negative that you see about your current situation. (Make sure you add this "decision to make this list" to your timeline too). Now focus and take a good look at the situation and if you can, make a note of every blessing in the midst of it, every time God extended grace. If you can see His hand in the middle of it, even if this is a season of reaping, I want you to make a conscious decision to correct yourself and redirect your thinking every time you get ready to complain. For a few days monitor your progress with this.

This is a little easier to do when it is a testing of your faith, because you know that God is getting ready to bless you tremendously when harvest time comes and because He needs to grow you for a new level. I want you to look real good at my story and see that even when we are disobedient, when He has a plan for your life, there is nothing anyone or anything can do to stop it and He will make sure you have everything you need to carry out your purpose and it requires longsuffering. He won't block everything because we would never learn so He will allow you to make mistakes. He wants to know you trust Him and can be faithful in believing what He said even when you cannot see it just as He is continuously faithful to us in spite of us.

PRAYER

Dear heavenly Father, we come thanking you not just for what you have done, are doing and getting ready to do, but for who you are. You are an amazing God, matchless God, awesome and mighty God. Lord I ask that you would forgive my sister or brother for anything they may have done, said or thought that was not like you and allow them to experience you Oh God in such a way that they might believe in the death, burial and resurrection of your son Jesus Christ so they too may be saved by grace and through faith as you said in your word. God I ask that you would be their comforter, friend, mind regulator, heart fixer, healer, provider, teacher, leader, guide, peace, center of their joy and way out of no way. Lord help them to acquire a teachable and obedient spirit. Endow them Oh God and give them a spirit of discernment to recognize your voice so that they may begin to take the necessary steps to follow you. Satan you have no authority or jurisdiction over their lives, family, finances, purpose, children, business, careers, health or relationship with God so I bind every demonic spirit, plot, ploy, plan and trick that you have formed and render it ineffective right now in the name of Jesus. No weapon formed against them shall prosper. They are more than conquerors through Jesus Christ and if He be for them, He is more than you and the world are against them. I claim healing and total liberation for them right now in

Jesus' name. I speak those things that are not as though they are and claim they are delivered right now according to their faith and are prospering in every area of life. I plead the blood of Jesus over every generational curse and every spirit of fear, doubt, depression, suicide, anger, bitterness, unforgiveness and vengeance. Lord I thank you in advance for every goal met and every success obtained and we will be careful to give you all the praise, glory and honor in Jesus' name, Amen.

NOTE: Make sure you are writing in your journal or recording your thoughts. Get it out.

STUDY SCRIPTURES:

Romans 8:24-28

Philippians 4:6

Ecclesiastes 7:9

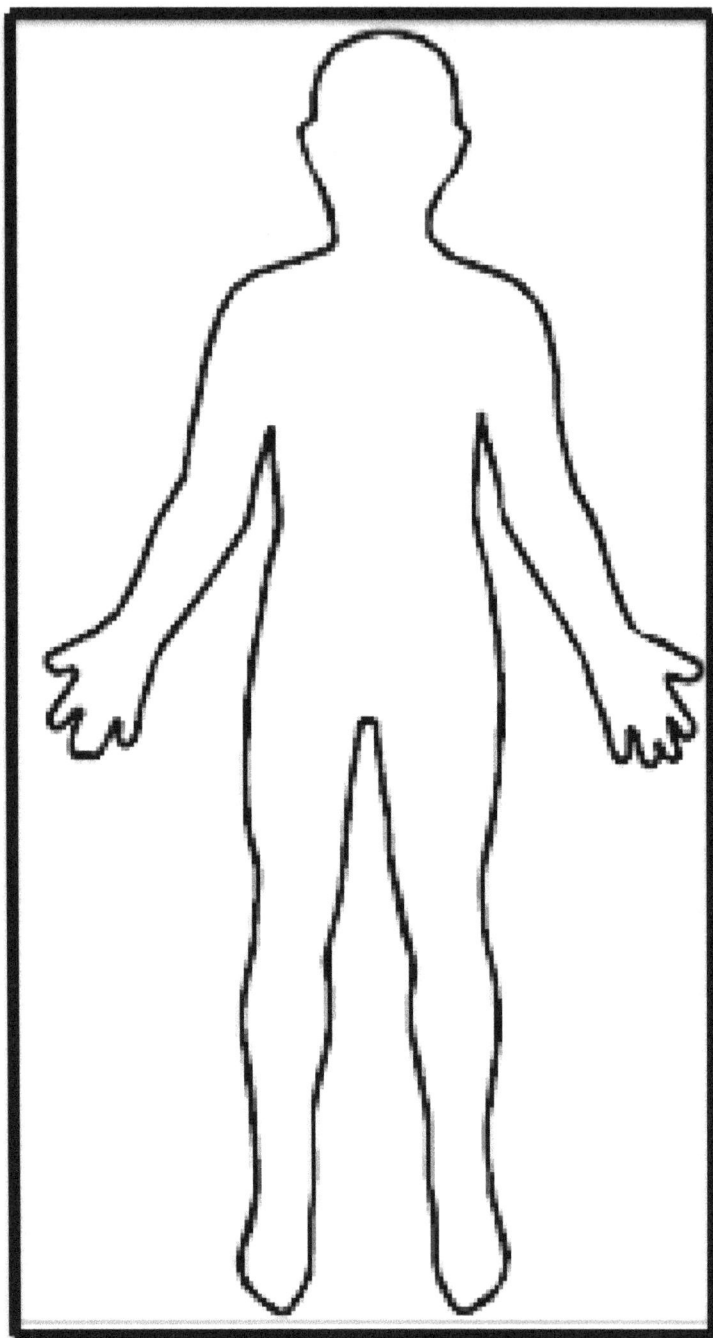

Chapter 3

INSTABILITY

Lack of firmness in weight bearing.

Dearly beloved, avenge not yourselves, but rather give place unto wrath: for it is written, Vengeance is mine; I will repay, saith the Lord (**Romans 12:19**).

Often times when people wrong us we expect immediate payment for what they have done. It is difficult to see our own behavior when we feel the magnitude of what others have done to us. We have to examine the role we may have played in the whole situation. It is also difficult to practice love and forgiveness when you are full of anger and bitterness. It always seems like we reap what we sow, while wrongdoers live blissfully and experience no repercussions. We must not forget that God's timing is not our timing and just because the reaping of their actions are not visible to you, doesn't mean they are not taking place. Our job is to love and forgive no matter what they may have done to us and let God handle it. When we try to seek revenge, it only makes the healing process longer and more difficult, because you end up getting yourself into much more trouble than you bargained for. Thank God there is no ditch deep enough that He cannot reach down and bring you out of. What a mighty God we serve!

Oftentimes, God has continued to bless me despite my failures. I am extremely grateful, but I couldn't seem to let go of the fact it seemed as if my ex-husband was getting away with his lack of responsibility. His poor parenting was causing me to suffer more. I continued to entertain him, my emotions were still up and down. I made one of the most drastic and dumbest decisions I ever made next.

I decided that I was tired of trying to do right all the time. I got tired of facing people that were cruel, nasty and blatantly disobeying God's word repeatedly. Yet, all the while everything in their

Uh oh! I am going into another relapse! I took 5 steps forward and 2 steps back. God wasn't moving fast enough for me.

lives seemed to be just peachy. I know I've never been perfect, but it seemed that no matter how hard I tried to do the right thing, I always ended up with the short end of the stick. I decided that for once in my life, I was going to rebel against God and do what I wanted to do. I became angry and just felt like life wasn't fair. Uh oh! I am going into another relapse! I took 5 steps forward and 2 steps back. God wasn't moving fast enough for me. Instead of focusing on me, I was still focusing on what my ex-husband was and "was not" doing.

In May 2007, I met a young man working at a store while I was shopping. I was a regular at this particular store and would see him often. I thought he was kind of weird at first until he opened his mouth and spoke to me. He stopped me while I was getting into my car. He was outside taking a smoke break. He asked me a few questions and requested my phone number. Now, I didn't date men that smoked, because I didn't smoke. I thought it was a complete turn off; nonetheless, I gave him my number anyway. I figured I was doing what I wanted to do, so what the heck.

We began dating and I started having feelings. He later discovered my feelings were only "rebound" feelings. We decided to get married in September 2007 at the Justice of Peace. On the way downtown, we argued because I told him that I didn't really want to marry him. He became furious and I gave in. I realized later that I had only done it to piss off my ex-husband. This was my "black-out" period, if you will. I was just doing things with no regard to others feelings or to the circumstances. I was way out of control! Complete relapse! I was finally walking, but now I just broke a leg.

We began to argue all the time. We argued about my ex-husband most of the time. He felt like I was still in love with him and that made him angry. He had some jealousy issues as well. We split up after a huge argument. He had put his hands around my arms and began to shake me very hard. I knew that he was capable of a lot worse, if things got heated enough. I realized I had gone from bad to worse. I began to tell and show him that I really didn't care for him that much and that I was with him on the rebound. I told him I only married him to make my ex-husband mad. I was out of control and way out of character! Towards the end of our relationship (which was extremely short), I slept with my ex-husband a few times as well. At first, it looked like my plan to teach him a lesson was working, but when I came to the realization that I was just hurting myself and someone else, I turned around and filed for an annulment.

In October 2007, I found out that I was pregnant. I was furious! I called him and told him that I didn't want the baby because I didn't want a baby with him. He tried to fling me through the front windshield of my van while we were on the highway. He intentionally and suddenly slammed on the brakes while we were arguing. His jealousy was out of control.

I began to have major issues with my pregnancy in December. The doctor made me quit my job due to the pregnancy being high risk. Also, I was working in a warehouse at the time. I was expected to have a miscarriage due to my condition. I was bleeding badly. By this time I had accepted the child. He had threatened to send a group of females to my house to jump me while I was pregnant with his child. I cut all ties from him and began only communicating with his younger sister and his mother. I was due to have the baby in July 2008.

I began collecting unemployment in January. I didn't qualify for FMLA. I decided that I would start trying to get my head together and try to get back on track once again. I struggled so hard as my need to be loved and feel wanted caused me to spiral out of control each time I experienced rejection.

Soon after, I started cosmetology school and began looking for a desk job. I began to see my ex-husband again and we tried to be cordial for the kids. My unemployment ran out and I found another job, but I was a month behind in rent. The manager wouldn't wait for me to get my first check. So, I lost my apartment. I moved back in with my ex-husband's mother. She wanted us there. She always checked on me. She still treated me like I was a part of the family and told me that I would always be. She became attached to the baby I was carrying as well. Later, she became an adopted grandmother and helped me out tremendously.

I found a good paying desk job and began to get back on track financially. I was still a little depressed about being pregnant by this man and about my life in general, but I just tried to take it one day at a time. I began having major complications. I started having panic attacks all the time, experienced high blood pressure, gestational diabetes and my amniotic fluid began to leak. Then reality hit me that I could lose the baby. I felt awful that the thought of abortion crossed my mind in the early stages. I chose to make the decision to put myself in a situation that I didn't want to be in. The baby had nothing to do with that. I was fully responsible.

I met a woman at work who used to be a member at my church and we became very good friends. For *Life Support* purposes, we'll call her Sharon. I explained what I was going through and told her that I didn't know how I was going to get everything the baby needed. I had given away all of my baby things to other people. It had been three years since my last child. She began treating me like a daughter and our friendship grew into much more – we became family.

Sharon got everyone together in our department at work and they all pitched in and got me absolutely everything I needed for the baby. They purchased a crib/playpen, swing, bouncer, clothes, shoes, bibs, blankets, car seat, etc. I didn't even have to buy a pack of diapers. I was overwhelmed with joy and began to cry. I couldn't express my gratitude enough. I asked her to be the baby's godmother. She accepted. I couldn't believe that once again, God had look beyond my faults and not only met my needs, but exceeded them, in spite of me. There He is again looking beyond my faults and several relapses! I began to get back on the right track. I began going back to church and doing what I knew was right. I knew there would be consequences to pay later and I already had a life-long consequence of being connected to the baby's father.

As I began trying to get back on track, my ex-husband and I began to fall out again and stopped speaking. Each time we would try to get past the past we got better and better, but then we would get knocked back a few steps. We both struggled with the ability to move forward and find common ground, but slowly and surely we were getting there.

The baby's father began harassing me. He would call my phone and hang up and leave threatening messages on my voicemail. Two days before I was due, I went downtown and got a restraining order. He was not to have any contact with the baby or me. On July 22, 2008, I gave birth to a beautiful baby girl. I thought I would give birth alone, but JR's mother, his sister, Sharon, and my mother were there. My mother was there for me for each of my children's births. We didn't speak often, but I always hoped that some form of consistent communication would form. I love my mother and thought very highly of her as a person, though I didn't agree with her decisions. Time will tell and only God knows what was in store for the future.

I received a call a couple of months later from someone telling me that my daughter's father had been locked up. I saw him shortly after she was born as he was granted supervised visitation once released from jail. After so long, those visits stopped and I didn't see him for a while. I saw him again on my daughters' first birthday. Afterward, we never saw him again. Looking back, I cannot believe how my anger, bitterness, resentment and hurt caused me to make decisions that led from bad to worse. I was in horrible shape and out of control. I was now a single mother of 3 children. I didn't have myself together mentally, spiritually or emotionally. I was determined to keep trying as I was responsible for teaching and leading 3 children.

CHAPTER 3 LESSON

Often times, we don't realize the domino effect of our behavior until it is too late. It is hard to see that our unwillingness to forgive can be toxic. The need for immediate justice or restitution causes erratic behavior that can have extremely bad consequences, as you read in my case. I was with someone I barely knew who had a jealous and violent side due to a bad temper. I cannot blame him for my part in the situation because he is only responsible for his actions. We must be able to step back and look at self and see where we went wrong and take responsibility. Though God allows us to make mistakes, it isn't always the bad things that happen as a result of our behavior that gets our attention. Sometimes it is His undeniable presence (hence the endless baby gifts I received in my case) in the midst of the chaos. It is His way of saying, "I am still here with you; just trust me." When you find yourself in a very dark place, pay attention to the light and follow that. We must not make decisions based solely on how we feel, because making permanent decisions based on temporary circumstances can have life-long consequences.

QUESTIONS

1.   What are some of the things and behaviors you notice in yourself that you constantly are exhibiting and are escalating?

_____

_____

_____

2.   What is causing you to spiral completely out of control and behave sporadically and out of character?

_____

_____

_____

3.   What has been some of the consequences of those behaviors and decisions? Do you want to change it?

_____

_____

ACTIVITIES

I want you to use the imperfect tree on page 50 and pretend you are the tree. Before something as beautiful and strong as a tree can blossom into what it is to become and bear fruit, it must first go through darkness, dirt, mud and many other changes before it can even see the sunlight. God makes each one individually great and allows it to take on a unique form but makes sure that during the growing phase, it has everything it needs. Some trees get "sick" when they aren't properly cared for due to lack of sunlight, water, etc. They need to be nursed back to health. Your tree or "you" are lacking what you need in order for you to produce fruit and before you reach self-destruction, you need to be nursed back to health.

Inside of the roots I want you to write the name or relation of the person you feel wronged you or an event that impacted you while using the deepest roots for those that you feel are at the core of how you feel, see yourself and behave. Leading up into the trunk, I want you to explain in just a few words of why they are one of the roots of your behavior. In the leaves I want you to write words that are a result (bitterness, anger, cold, lack of trust, etc.). In the last book of this series, we will see how your new tree will look once the leaves on this one begin falling off and is uprooted because we know that God makes all things new! This is another exercise to see yourself now in the height of your chaos. Look at how many leaves are filled in and how many roots are filled in. Notice there is no fruit on the tree. Eventually it will wither and die. Self-destruction is not an option. Failure is not an option. Lack of progress and production is not an option.

NOTE: Make sure you are writing in your journal or recording your thoughts. Get it out.

STUDY SCRIPTURES:

James 4:17

Romans 7:15

Romans 12:21

Galatians 6:7-10

1 Corinthians 10:13

Chapter 4

DYSPRAXIA

*Deficient motor planning that is
often related to a decrease in sensory processing.*

See then that ye walk circumspectly, not as fools, but as wise, redeeming the time, because the days are evil. Wherefore be ye not unwise, but understanding what the will of the Lord is (**Ephesians 5:15-17**).

There may have been times and/or will be times when we ask God for clarity. He usually gives it to us, and we often ignore it. We see all types of red flags and consistent hazard zones, but we proceed anyway, thinking we can handle it, change it, or change somebody. We lack wisdom and understanding and as a result, we find ourselves back at square one. Putting aside our own will to follow His will and instructions would save us the time, pain and energy of having to rebuild from a forced demolition. Instead, we build non-sturdy structures from the beginning. It is much wiser to wait on God, use the tools and materials He equips us with, and follow instructions. Moving forward with limits is pointless. You will not get very far.

At this point, I haven't gotten very far in my *Rehab,* but I am not where I was before. It will get worse before it gets better. I may need an intervention from the most High God - let's see.

My ex-husband and I were back on good terms and were doing so well. We had our spats here and there but each time we got better. I was now a single mother of three. Two months after I gave birth, I met a man named Alfred. He was a member at my church and had been a member there for a year. I never recognized him nor did I remember passing him the hallways. For some odd reason, we kept running into each other. He told me that he knew my son and that my son spoke to him at church every time he saw him. We exchanged numbers and I never called.

A few weeks had passed and I found an apartment and planned to move in November of 2008. I called one of the deacons at the church to see if he could help me move. Ironically, he recommended that I call Alfred. I called him and asked if he would help me move. He said yes. We began to talk and date. He instantly took to my children and became a father to my 2 month old. He claimed her as his own.

A week after moving into my apartment, I discovered that it had a severe pest problem. I addressed the issue with management and they told me they would take care of it. I never unpacked my belongings. The majority of my things I took back to storage. The problem was so severe that I couldn't keep food in the house and all 3 of my children stayed in my bedroom. We ate out all the time or at other's houses. I even had to stay with my sister for a week so they could fix the problem. It never did get fixed, so I asked them to refund my money. I found out that other brand new tenants had the same problem. They filed lawsuits when the property refused to refund their money.

Alfred and I continued dating and I really started to develop feelings for him. He was sweet, kind, funny, handsome, saved, and most of all, a gentleman. I knew that I was over my ex-husband when Alfred had my complete undivided attention. I no longer cared what my ex-husband was doing or who he was with. He wasn't sinking his claws in me anymore. I explained the situation between us to Alfred and he understood.

Alfred and I began to be intimate. Uh oh! Here I go again! I am allowing my emotions to control me. I became pregnant when my daughter was 5 months old. I was distraught. I wasn't able to make it to the clinic to get a morning after pill due to the fact that I had to go to work. I didn't know what to do. I knew I couldn't possibly carry a child to full term this time since I now had Uterine Prolapse. I had the same issue with my 3rd child, but after giving birth it was worse. Even though I didn't believe

Uh oh! Here i go again! I am allowing my emotions to control me. I became pregnant when my daughter was 5 months old.

in abortions, I told Alfred that I was going to have an abortion the same day I found out that I was pregnant. He became furious and he stormed out and I didn't see or talk to him for three days.

Three days later, I finally ran into him at the church and we began to argue. I asked him where had he been and he wouldn't tell me. I asked him several times if he was with another female and he replied, "No." I told him that I decided to keep the baby. We were doing fine for a while. By the end of December, I was having major complications. I was bleeding very heavily. I was unable to function regularly on a daily basis. I was in a lot of pain, and having other complications. My uterine prolapse was at its worst. The doctors told me that if I decided to carry to full term, there was a 70% chance that I could bleed out. This was a very difficult decision, but I had to take into account that I had 3 other children that needed me alive. That wasn't to say that my unborn child's life was worth less. Once again I made decisions that put me in a position that I wasn't prepared to handle. There goes God showing me myself again! I tried to keep the baby as long as I could. I didn't even make the final decision to have an abortion until I was 2 weeks into my 2nd trimester. Yes, my 2nd trimester. I told Alfred that I had to get an abortion. He didn't agree and he wasn't happy about it, but he stuck with me. I couldn't take it anymore. A week before Valentine's Day, he took me to the abortion clinic.

HABITUATION: *The neurological process of tuning out familiar sensations.*

I walked into the clinic scared and trembling. My heart was racing. My eyes almost jumped out of my head when I saw how many teenagers, young women, and middle-aged women were getting abortions. I ran into a high school friend of mine who worked there and she told me that it was packed like that every day. There were people sitting outside the door in the hallway. That's how packed it was. There were also abortion protesters all in front of the building outside. It took everything in me to hold back my tears. I talked with a few of the girls in the waiting area and I learned that some of them visit the abortion clinic on a regular. Some of them had been there 3, 4, and 5 times. I thought that was just ridiculous. You would think that after the first time, they would wrap it up or become abstinent, especially if they're adamant about not having children.

It was my turn. I went into a room where they gave me an ultrasound to determine how far along I was. My baby was into the second trimester. That's how long it took me to make a decision. My baby had all of his or her body parts. He or she was just a smaller version of a full term child. Pastor White's voice came into my head and said, "Abortion is murder." I remember him saying that in a sermon a few years prior. I tried so hard not to think about that. I couldn't think of myself as a murderer. I thought about the ultrasound in the emergency room a few weeks before. The baby was punching with clenched fists like it was swinging at a punching bag. Alfred said, "Look! You can't get an abortion. The baby is fighting to live." This broke my heart. I kept thinking about what the doctor said about me miscarrying and maybe bleeding out during labor if I made it into the third trimester. I kept thinking about the pain I was in and the high risk of the pregnancy. My blood pressure began to rise. I wasn't on any blood pressure medicine, so I tried to calm myself down.

After taking a small pill, it was my turn to go into the procedure room. I entered the procedure room and asked the nurse if I could change my mind. She told me that it was too late since I had taken the pill to begin cramps or contractions and to soften my cervix. She left me in the room alone. I sat in the room in complete silence. The doctor and the nurse walked into the room and saw the horror in my eyes and told me to relax. He began to explain and show me what he was getting ready to do. He detailed the procedure and showed me how the machine and tools worked. He assured me that it wouldn't be painful, but little did he know, I was in excruciating pain already on the inside. I laid back in the chair/table and closed my eyes. He inserted a tool and started the vacuum. As soon as I heard the vacuum come on, I opencd my eyes and tears began to roll down my face. Inside, I was yelling; Stop! Stop! Stop! But my mouth wasn't moving. Nothing was coming out. I tried not to let them see me crying.

When the doctor was finished, he left the room. The nurse told me that I could put my clothes back on. She left the room. I sat up and noticed there was a little window in the wall across from me with a door. The door was open. I don't believe the nurse was supposed to leave it open. Inside, sitting on the little shelf was a tray with my 13-week old baby wrapped in a blue cloth. I was frozen with guilt, horror, sadness, anger, and regret. I began to cry even more. I wanted to go over and put my baby back together and hold him or her. I couldn't believe what I had just done. I asked them to stop, but it was too late. I managed to get my clothes back on. The nurse walked into the room and escorted me to the recovery area.

Every female sitting in the recovery area showed no regret or emotion about what they had just done, at least not to the blind eye. I couldn't get myself together. Recovery was only supposed to last for 5-10 minutes. They checked my vital signs, gave me some cookies, provided medicine, instructed me to sign some papers, and sent me home. That was it. It was taking everything in me to hold back my tears publically. The nurse delayed my departure, checking my blood pressure 3 times before I was released. I was so distraught that my blood pressure was extremely high. After about 45 minutes, I was able to gather myself and they allowed me leave.

I went through the lobby area to the door and didn't see Alfred. I went outside and there he was sitting in his car. He told me that he couldn't stay in that place. I didn't say a word. I sat back in my seat and turned my head towards the window and didn't utter a sound. He started the car and drove off the lot. We were on our way to the church. He had to speak with someone. The whole way there, neither of us said anything and I kept my face toward the window and cried silently. When we arrived at the church, one of my trusted friends came outside and asked me how I was feeling. I looked up at her and broke down. I was crying hysterically. She wrapped her arms around me and told me that it was going to be alright.

Two weeks later, Alfred and I began to become angrier at each other at times. We would argue all the time about him cheating. He would swear that he wasn't doing anything, but I knew better. He was still angry with me for having the abortion. One morning while getting ready for work, I heard his phone chirp. It was about 5:00 a.m. It was a text message from a girl telling him that she was pregnant, and he was the father. I couldn't believe what I was seeing. I woke him up. "What the hell is this," I asked? He began to answer but I interrupted him. "I asked you if you were with anyone else and you told me no. I was just pregnant with your child and just got an abortion and now some chick is texting you, telling you she's pregnant? I don't want to hear your excuse, just get out" I screamed. He grabbed my arms and begged me to listen. He told me that he was with her for those 3 days he went missing in December. I couldn't believe what I was hearing. I couldn't believe this was happening again. I was back in the same position I was with my ex-husband. On top of that, I just killed my own child. I was struggling trying to make it through rehab but my emotions and the enemy knows my weak spots. It doesn't look like I will ever be strong enough to get to the graduation phase.

Even though he hurt me, I still loved and cared for him. After a while, we were back on okay terms. We were intimate once again. A few weeks later, I was pregnant again. I told myself I wouldn't go through another abortion. Alfred got angry when I told him that I was pregnant again. He accused me of getting pregnant on purpose. We stopped speaking again. Our friends, Erica and Tony tried to counsel us and give us tips on what to do in situations like ours since they had been through it before. It was no use though because things still didn't get better.

In May 2009, I lost my job. I was unable to pay rent, car payment, and other bills because of this. I went to the church to ask for food from the pantry to feed my children. I began creating a "Strength Wall." I chose a section in my apartment to put up motivational and encouraging scriptures, songs, and sermon excerpts. This got me through the hard days. I tried to stay faithful in my walk with God, continued to go to church, and continued in the choir ministry. I knew that I had to reap what I sowed. I just had an abortion and I knew that wasn't what God intended. I knew that He would show up soon and that He would get me through it.

The manager tried to work with me and hold off on evicting me so that I could find some assistance. I was unable to come up with the money or find a job. In July, I told Alfred that I was being evicted and asked if we could stay with him a night or two until I found somewhere to go. He replied, "No." That topped the cake for me. I'm a single mother of three children and 2 months pregnant with his child and he didn't care if I was on the street. First red flag, but I proceeded anyway!

I ended up staying at a hotel with my children for a week then slept wherever we could day to day for about 4 days. I swallowed my pride and called around to some shelters. All the shelters only had room for an adult with 1 to 2 children. Some shelters were on a first come first serve basis. I couldn't allow my children to be split up and I couldn't allow them to live from place to place. So, I sent out a text to about 7 people that I knew and trusted asking them for help. None of them knew of a place, but they did try and help me find somewhere to go.

I got a phone call from a member of my church choir. She heard of my ordeal through one of my friends and offered to let us stay with her until I was able to get my own apartment. I was overwhelmed with relief and gratitude. I couldn't thank her enough.

Tanisha was a very kind and sweet person and she just loved my children. She had a daughter of her own. She was so good to us and helped me out while we were staying there. I had begun looking for a job. I started working for a temporary service, but the assignment didn't last long. My van broke down. The engine quit on me. I started getting frustrated, but I had to tell myself that wasn't going to do any good. In spite of my circumstances, I was still determined to keep going, and I didn't care what others thought.

After a while, I found another job and began making enough money to begin looking for a place to stay. It was the beginning of September and I received a phone call from a member of the church who managed some apartments. She asked me if I was still looking for a place to stay. I replied, "Yes." She got me approved and told me that I could move in at the end of September. I told Tanisha the good news and thanked her for all she had done. I told her that I was eternally grateful because she didn't have to do what she did. We moved into our new apartment September 28, 2009. There he goes again stepping in and showing grace when I didn't deserve it!

Alfred and I went back and forth for a while and as I became further along in my pregnancy, he began to be more involved. At about 5 months, I was having trouble with my pregnancy. My baby wasn't breathing normally and they could never get a heartbeat on the monitor. I had an ultrasound every time I went to the doctor to check his heart rate. I also got my blood pressure checked often, because I was starting to have signs of eclampsia.

By this time, my ex-husband and I had a very long conversation that finally gave us both closure as we were able to forgive one another and move forward in trying to work together for our children. Alfred and I began living together and preparing for the arrival of the baby. On February 24, 2010, I gave birth to a beautiful baby boy. In October of 2010, Alfred and I were married. It seemed like a fresh start and I could finally get on with the rest of my *Rehab*.

God had been tugging at me to start giving back and helping others by using my testimony. I had already been active in helping to serve the homeless through my church. He had much more in store for me. He laid the book *Life Support* on my heart and I began writing May 2010. I had the whole first part of the series written in 2 weeks! Looking back now, little did I know He was showing me the cracks in my foundation and mistakes I was currently making at the time. God was trying to get me to stay focused on Him, but I missed it.

Things were great for a while. I started a nonprofit organization to help single parents, teens and the homeless. It was incorporated in the state of Indiana July 2010. I went back to school to get my business management degree and the nonprofit was taking off so fast. Things started to get rocky in 2011 and I began experiencing arguments more frequently, infidelity and physical abuse. Alfred did have a bad temper and for some reason jealousy and assumptions caused him to blow up. He hit me a couple of times and choked me once and I fought back. I was fed up. I was a mother of 4, founder/president of a nonprofit, full time student and worked part time. I was also dealing with severe marital issues at home.

I was determined that no matter what happened from this point on, I would not make the same mistakes again. Once I decided I wanted a divorce, I found out that our house, cars, other bills, office, etc. were all in default due in part to our money being used to satisfy selfish lustful desires with other women. I was with the same company for 3 years and was being evicted, both cars were repossessed, was also evicted from the business office, and all the utilities were disconnected. I was completely blindsided and everything I worked hard for was gone in the blink of an eye.

DIRECTIONALITY: *The awareness of right/left, forward/back, and up/down, and the ability to move oneself in those directions.*

I couldn't believe that I had just lost everything. I stepped outside of myself and began looking for his gun. I remember calling my pastor and telling him I was going to kill my husband. All of the money was gone and I had absolutely nowhere to go with my children. I had just hit rock bottom, but when you are at the bottom, the only way to go from there is up. If you continue ignoring what God is trying to tell you and show you, He has a way of making you pay attention.

Use the tools, tips and activities daily or weekly to help you through your healing and forgiveness stages. Start taking your life back one day at a time. It's not easy but it is worth it. It gets better and each day gets sweeter.

So how did I go from making all those mistakes during the first part of the *Rehab* phase, to finally reaching a little stability? And then after getting my life in order to losing everything again, to getting back to where I am now? How did I lose everything even down to our clothes, shoes, all furniture and other belongings? I still was not fully healed or emotionally stable and still came out better, stronger and wiser? How did I go from having to start completely over from scratch with my children to obtaining another degree, am now the owner/operator of 2 companies and founder/president of a nonprofit and an author? How did I come to love and like me totally and completely? How did I enter into total liberation and exceed every expectation, prove every underestimation wrong and persevere through it all relentlessly with no more vicious cycles?

You must stay tuned for the finale of the series *Life Support* and see what happened right after this and how I got to where I am today! I know you want the details now. Go through your *Rehab* and don't relapse as many times as I did. In the next book we will cover how to finally reach the end of the healing phase. Afterward, we will hit the ground running to start taking back everything the enemy stole. Let's Get It! *Life Support: I'm Possible* is the finale!

CHAPTER 1 LESSON

Sometimes it seems that we have grasped the concept of being able to move forward. We think we are ready and once we realize that we're not, instead of stopping and regrouping, we keep going in hopes that things will get better or change. This can lead to a raggedy mess as you read about in my life's story. We must remember that there are signs along the journey for a reason and a manual is given for directions. You would not step on the gas in a car if you were approaching a red light. So, why would we do that in life? If God places caution signs along the road that means it isn't the path He chose for you. We must be mindful that although a path looks more difficult and less fun than the one we would much rather take, it will lead to a dead end. We must ask ourselves, how bad do I want it and what am I willing to do and give up to get there? Staying focused on the "Why" will drive your motivation behind the "What" while God takes care of the "How."

QUESTIONS:

1.   At what point did you realize you hit rock bottom?

_____

_____

_____

2.   What is the main reason you must succeed?

_____

_____

_____

3.   What and/or who do you feel has the ability to keep you from your Freedom, Healing, Purpose and Prosperity? (if applicable) Why?

_____

_____

_____

ACTIVITIES

1. Get a notepad. On each sheet, write down a word (in large capital letters) of what you still need to uproot and get rid of. As you are writing, I want you to think about how it has controlled your life by consuming your every thought and keeping you stagnant. Let the emotions flow. Imagine that as you are writing each word, (guilt, shame, abandonment, low self-esteem, etc.) it is leaving your body.

Now get a trash can and tear each paper from the notebook one by one and begin putting it in the trash as you recite each one with these words following it "_____, NO MORE!" You may also dig a hole outside and bury all of it and plant a flower on top as the most heart-wrenching, ugly and shameful things produce the most beautiful things in our lives. You may also use a grill or fire pit and burn each sheet.

2. Build you a strength wall. Chose a section or wall in your home to put up motivational and encouraging scriptures, quotes, songs, and sermon excerpts on construction paper or place in plaques and hang them all on one wall. As you begin your journey through the healing process, the enemy will try everything in his power to get you to revert back to old habits and behaviors and will use your weaknesses to keep you stuck and unable to move forward. Add to your wall daily or whenever you feel needed. Stand in front of that wall as often as you would like and speak those things into your spirit. Speak those things that are not as though they are. Win the battle in your mind first and your actions will follow. As you move forward in your *Rehab* process, each time you feel yourself going backwards, having a bad day, reverting back to old thinking, see that your timeline and mirror reflection is not changing

stand in front of that wall and just begin speaking it into yourself again and believe what you speak. There will come a time when you won't need to stand in front of it anymore because it will all be deeply rooted in you to begin the planting of a new tree to bear much fruit!

NOTE: Make sure you are writing in your journal or recording your thoughts. Get it out.

STUDY SCRIPTURES:

Proverbs 3:5-6

Proverbs 12:15

James 4:7

MY REHAB JOURNAL

MY REHAB JOURNAL

_____

_____

_____

_____

_____

_____

_____

_____

_____

_____

MY REHAB JOURNAL

_____

_____

_____

_____

_____

_____

_____

_____

_____

_____

MY REHAB JOURNAL

_____

_____

_____

_____

_____

_____

_____

_____

_____

_____

MY REHAB JOURNAL

MY REHAB JOURNAL

MY REHAB JOURNAL

MY REHAB JOURNAL

_____

_____

_____

_____

_____

_____

_____

_____

_____

_____

_____

_____

MY REHAB JOURNAL

MY REHAB JOURNAL

_____

_____

_____

_____

_____

_____

_____

CONTACT:

Author Jacquie Murrell
LIFE SUPPORT COMPANY
_"Helping others transition from resuscitation
to releasein all areas of life!"_

www.lifesupportmurrell.webs.com
www.facebook.com/jacquiemurrell
317-886-0296
1-888-689-3066 ext. 2

www.ingramcontent.com/pod-product-compliance
Lightning Source LLC
Chambersburg PA
CBHW060144050426
42448CB00010B/2282